FAST CARS

Frances Ridley

Editorial Consultant – Cliff Moon

RISING ★ STARS

nasen
NASEN House, 4/5 Amber Business Village, Amber Close, Amington, Tamworth, Staffordshire B77 4RP

Rising Stars UK Ltd.
22 Grafton Street, London W1S 4EX
www.risingstars-uk.com

Every effort has been made to trace copyright holders and obtain their permission for use of copyright material. The publisher will gladly receive information enabling them to rectify any error or omission in subsequent editions. All facts are correct at time of going to press.

Published 2006
Reprinted 2006

Cover design: Button plc
Cover image: Ilianski / Alamy
Illustrator: Bill Greenhead
Text design and typesetting: Nicholas Garner, Codesign
Technical adviser: Mark Rendes
Educational consultants: Cliff Moon and Lorraine Petersen
Pictures: Motoring Picture Library/NMM; pages 4, 5, 6, 7, 9, 10, 11, 12, 14, 18, 19, 20, 21, 22, 23, 26, 29, 31, 32, 33, 38, 43: Getty Images; page 7: Alamy; pages 5, 6, 8, 9, 13, 14, 15, 18, 20, 22, 26, 27, 28, 30, 39, 40, 41.

British Library Cataloguing in Publication Data.
A CIP record for this book is available from the British Library.

ISBN: 978-1-905056-95-8
Printed by Craft Print International Ltd, Singapore

Contents

Sports cars

Most fast cars are sports cars.

Sports cars have good **acceleration** and they have good top speeds.

Sports cars **handle** well. They are good at **cornering** and braking.

Coupes

A coupe is a sports car with a fixed roof.

A Maserati 3200GT coupe

Convertibles

A convertible has a roof that folds away.

Convertibles have side windows that roll up.

A Mercedes CLK430 convertible

Roadsters

A roadster is a two-seater convertible.

Most roadsters are light-weight sports cars.

A Nissan 350Z roadster

Supercars and hot hatches

Supercars

Supercars are **high-performance** sports cars.
They cost a lot of money.

Supercars can go from 0 mph to 60 mph in 5 seconds.

Supercars can have top speeds of 220 mph.

The McLaren F1 goes from 0 mph to 60 mph in 3.2 seconds.

The Ferrari Enzo goes from 0 mph to 100 mph in 6.5 seconds.

Hot hatches

'Hot hatches' are fast **hatchback** cars.

They have good acceleration and good top speeds.

They do not cost as much as sports cars.

The Mini Cooper S is a hot hatch.

Making and selling fast cars

Making fast cars

Different things make a car fast.

This is the Porsche 911:

- It has a powerful engine.
- It is light-weight.
- It has a **streamlined** shape.
- It has a **rear-mounted engine.**

Porsche 911/997

Selling fast cars

Fast cars are sold under brand names. These brand names are called marques.

Many marques have a link with racing cars – this is good for sales.

Ferarri make racing cars and fast cars for the road.

Each marque has a symbol:

Mercedes Benz 300SL

Mercedes Benz is a German company.

The symbol is a star with three points.

These points stand for land, sea and air.

Mercedes Benz made engines for cars, boats and planes.

The 300SL was made from 1954 to 1963.

It was made as a coupe and a roadster.

The 300SL roadster

The 300SL has a **fuel-injection** petrol engine. It was the first road car to have this.

Top speed	165 mph
0-60 mph	9 seconds
Miles per gallon	18 mpg

The coupe was called the 'gullwing'.

Its doors look like wings when they are open.

The 'gullwing' coupe

Jaguar E-Type

Jaguar is a British company.

Its symbol is a jaguar. The cars are fast and powerful – like big cats.

Jaguar started in 1922. It has always made **classic** cars.

The Jaguar XK120 was made in 1948 but it still looks good today!

The E-Type was made from 1961 to 1975.

It looked good. It was fast and powerful. It **handled** well and it did not cost as much as other sports cars!

The E-Type was a big hit for Jaguar and 70,000 E-Types were sold.

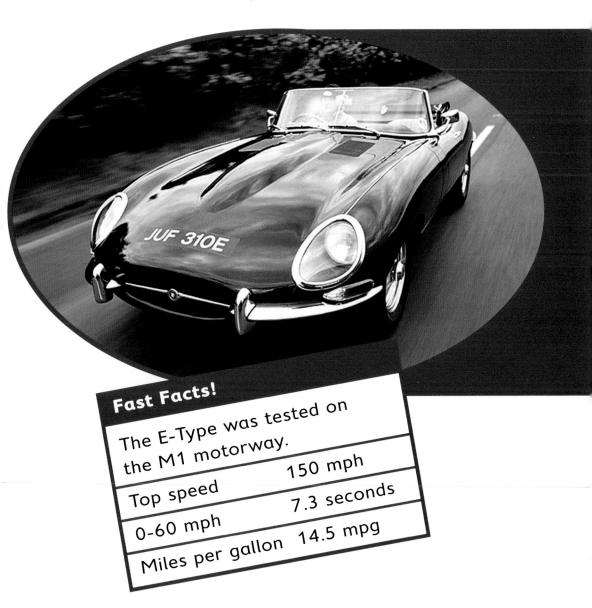

Fast Facts!

The E-Type was tested on the M1 motorway.

Top speed	150 mph
0-60 mph	7.3 seconds
Miles per gallon	14.5 mpg

Chevrolet Corvette Sting Ray 1963

Chevrolet cars are made by
an American company.

The Chevrolet Corvette Sting Ray was made in 1963.

The 1963 Sting Ray is a coupe

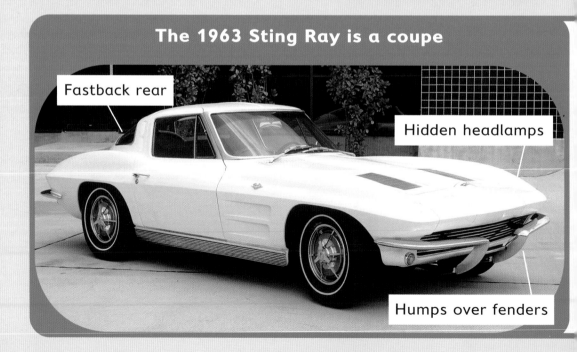

Fastback rear

Hidden headlamps

Humps over fenders

The Chevrolet Corvette Sting Ray was a big hit. 21,000 Sting Rays were made in 1963!

Top speed	118 mph
0-60 mph	6.1 seconds
Miles per gallon	18 mpg

Split back window

The Sting Ray had a split back window.

Some people said this was not safe.

The 1964 Sting Ray had a normal back window.

Dream Car (Part one)

"That car is so lush!" said Moz.

Rashid nodded. "It's a dream car," he said.

A shout made them jump. It was Mr Green.

"Hey!" he said. "Get lost!"

"We're just looking, Mr Green," said Rashid.

"Look at something else!" he said. "You put people off."

Just then, a woman came in. She had long blonde hair. She was very smart.

"How can I help you?" said Mr Green.

"My name is Helen Preston. I need a car," she said. "The Aston looks good."

"Come this way," said Mr Green.

"I've seen that woman before," said Moz.

"She's rich," said Rashid. "Maybe she's famous. Maybe you've seen her on TV."

"Maybe," said Moz. "Come on, help me with my paper round, Rashid!"

Continued on page 24

Lamborghini Miura

Lamborghini is an Italian company.

Lamborghini cars have smooth, sweeping shapes.

The Diablo

The Murcielago

Lamborghini's symbol is a charging bull.

Many Lamborghini cars have names
to do with bullfighting.

The Miura was Lamborghini's first car and it put Lamborghini on the map.

The Miura was the first road car with a **mid-mounted** engine.

All modern Lamborghinis have **mid-mounted** engines.

The Miura has a very sleek shape.

Fast Facts!

The open doors of the Miura look like a bull's horns.

Top speed	172 mph
0-60 mph	6.9 seconds
Miles per gallon	11.2 mpg

Volkswagen Golf GTi

Volkswagen is a German company.

It is one of the biggest car companies in the world.

In 1976 VW made the Golf GTi. It was a Golf car with a **fuel-injection engine**.

The car sold very well, as more people wanted small, sporty **hatchbacks**.

There have been five **generations** of Golf GTi cars.

Mk5 Golf GTi

WOB CP 440

Fast Fact!

The Volkwagen Golf GTi was the first hot hatch!

Top speed	146 mph
0-60 mph	7.2 seconds
Miles per gallon	34.9 mpg

Ferrari F40

Ferrari is an Italian company.

Its symbol is a **prancing** horse. It was the symbol of a World War One air force hero.

Ferrari is famous for its **styling**.

Ferrari Testarossa

D73 WPA

The car's name means red head.
The top of its engine is painted red.

Ferrari F40

Large wing

Deep scoops

The Ferrari F40 was made to mark Enzo Ferrari's 40th birthday.

Ferrari wanted to make a Formula One car for the road.

The Ferrari F40 was the first **road legal** 200 mph car.

Many people think it was the first supercar.

1315 cars were made from 1987 to 1992.

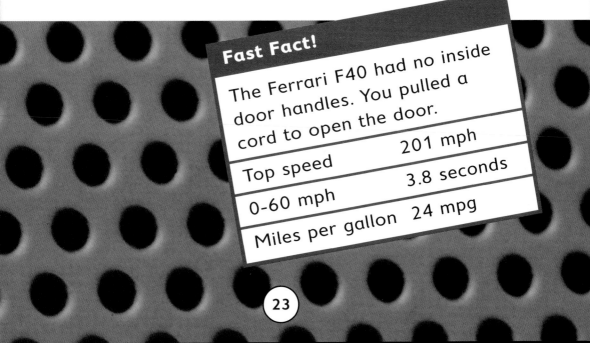

Fast Fact!

The Ferrari F40 had no inside door handles. You pulled a cord to open the door.

Top speed	201 mph
0-60 mph	3.8 seconds
Miles per gallon	24 mpg

Dream Car (Part two)

The paper round did not take long.

"Oh no!" said Rashid.

"What's the matter?" said Moz.

"I had a letter to post for Mum," said Rashid.
"I left it at Green's."

They went back to Green's. The letter was
still there.

"That's good," said Rashid. "Let's go and post it."

The boys got on their bikes. Then Betty
came out. She worked for Mr Green.

"Is Mr Green back yet?" she asked. "He went with Miss Preston on a test drive. They've been gone a long time."

"They'll be back soon," said Rashid.

"Yes, but it's odd," said Betty. "He took both sets of keys for the Aston."

She went back inside.

"That *is* odd," said Moz.

"Whatever," said Rashid. "Let's go and post Mum's letter."

Continued on page 34

McLaren F1

McLaren Cars is a British company.
The F1 was its first road car.

The F1 is a three-seat coupe.
The driver sits in the middle.

The McLaren F1 GTR won the 1995 Le Mans race.

Fast Facts!

Each McLaren F1 took 2250 hours to make.
The inside of the engine bay is made of gold.

Top speed	231 mph
0-60 mph	3.1 seconds
Miles per gallon	12.4 mpg

Only 100 McLaren F1 cars were made.

A new F1 cost more than any other road car but every car lost money for the company.

Renault
Clio Williams

Renault is a French company.

Its symbol is a diamond.
The symbol was first used on the 40 CV.

L'AUTOMOBILE EN 1925

The 40 CV

LA RENAULT

The Renault Clio Williams was made in 1995.

The car was named after Williams F1. Renault made the engines for this team.

Only 400 cars were made.

The Clio Williams is a hot hatch. It is very fast for a small car and it **handles** very well.

Fast Facts!

Clio Williams cars are all blue. They have gold wheels.	
Top speed	135 mph
0-60 mph	7.8 seconds
Miles per gallon	25 mpg

Porsche Boxster

Porsche is a German company.

Porsche cars are good for everyday use.

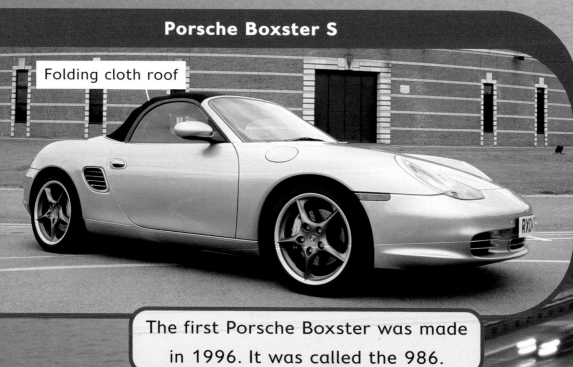

Porsche Boxster S

Folding cloth roof

The first Porsche Boxster was made in 1996. It was called the 986.

Porsche still make the Boxster today.

The Boxster is a small roadster that drives well and doesn't cost too much money.

It is a big seller for Porsche.

Lots of trunk and hood space

Fast Facts!

In 1955, the actor James Dean died in a crash in his Porsche 550 Spyder. In 2002, Porsche made the James Dean Edition Boxster. It looked like Dean's Spyder – silver with a brown canvas roof.

Top speed	149 mph
0-60 mph	6.9 seconds
Miles per gallon	23.5 mpg

Lotus Elise

Lotus is a British company.

It used to make Formula One cars.

Lotus cars are small and fast.

Lotus Esprit Turbo

Lotus Elan

Fast Facts!

'Elise' was the name of the Lotus chairman's grandchild.	
Top speed	124 mph
0-60 mph	5.5 seconds
Miles per gallon	29.4 mpg

The Lotus Elise was made in 1995.

It is an open sports car.

The Elise has a small engine but good **acceleration**.

It is good at **cornering** because it is very light-weight.

The Lotus Elise weighs only 724 kg.

Other sports cars are much heavier than this.

Dream Car (Part three)

The boys biked into town. The lights were red.

A big box van pulled up beside the boys.
Moz looked up at the driver.

"Hey Rashid! Follow that van!" he shouted.

They sped after the van. It went out of town.
It pulled into Farm Road.

Farm Road was a dead end. The boys went past
it and pulled over. Moz was writing a number
onto his hand.

"What is it?" said Rashid.

"The woman in the van," said Moz. "She works at the supermarket."

"So what?" said Rashid.

"She was the woman at Green's. But she had a wig on then."

"So what?" said Rashid.

"She must have the Aston in that van! That's why both keys were gone."

Moz called the police on his mobile. He was right.

Continued on the next page

The woman had taken the other key. Mr Green had taken her out for lunch and then the woman took the car.

Moz told the police the van's number and where it was.

The police came fast and they had Mr Green with them.

The police went to arrest the woman.

Mr Green stayed with the boys.

"I want to thank you two," he said. "You're not so bad, after all. How about a ride back in the Aston?"

"Cool!" shouted Rashid and Moz.

DREAM CAR SAFE AND SOUND!

Two teenagers stopped a car thief yesterday. Mr Green said: 'These boys are heroes. Their fast thinking saved a fast car!'

Aston Martin Vanquish

Aston Martin belongs to the Ford Motor Company.

The cars are made in Britain.

The symbol is a pair of wings.

The Vanquish S

The Aston Martin V12 Vanquish is a **flagship** car.

It was made in 2001 and was Aston Martin's fastest road car.

The Vanquish was updated in 2005. The new car is called the Vanquish S.

Pagani Zonda C12-S

Pagani is an Italian company.

Horacio Pagani always wanted to make supercars.

He made his first F3 racing car when he was 20.

Pagani started his company in 1999.
The Zonda was its first car.

Pointed nose

Flaps

The Zonda's shape is very streamlined.

Fast Facts!

Only 25 Zondas are made each year.
You have to order a Zonda.
You can pick the wheels, tyres and colours that you want.
You get a pair of shoes with the car. The shoe leather is the same as the seat leather.

0-60 mph	3.7 seconds
Top speed	220 mph
Miles per gallon	13 mpg

Koenigsegg CRR

Koenigsegg are a Swedish company.

Koenigsegg had a fire in their factory and had to move to another building.

Swedish Fighter Jets used to be kept in the new building. The Fighter Jets' symbol was a ghost.

The CRR is made in this building.

It has the same ghost symbol.

The CRR was made in 2004.

Fast Facts!

The CRR is a hardtop but you can take the roof panel off. The panel fits under the front hood.

Top speed	241 mph
0-60 mph	3.1 seconds

Curved windscreen

Air intake

The CRR is very **streamlined**.

Quiz

1 What kind of roof does a convertible have?

2 What is a marque?

3 Why is the Mercedes Benz coupe called the 'gullwing'?

4 What famous road was the Jaguar E-Type tested on?

5 What is Lamborghini's symbol?

6 What was the first hot hatch car?

7 How many seats does the McLaren F1 have?

8 What colour are the wheels on a Renault Clio Williams?

9 What is the top speed for a Lotus Elise?

10 How many seconds does the Pagani Zonda take to go from 0 to 60 mph?

Glossary of terms

acceleration	A change in speed.
active camouflage	Panels that can change colour – they let an object blend in with the background.
classic	Does not date – a classic car still looks good today.
cornering	Going round corners.
flagship car	A company's most important car.
fuel-injection engine	An engine that has fuel pushed into it – it makes the engine more powerful.
generations	Some cars are sold for many years. They are updated every few years. Each group of updated cars is called a generation.
handling	How easy the car is to drive. A car handles well if it is easy to steer and brake.
hatchback	A car with a door that goes all the way across the back. The door pulls up to open.
high-performance	A car that has good top speeds and acceleration.
mid-mounted engine	An engine in the middle of the car.
prancing	Moving with high steps.
rear-mounted engine	An engine at the back of the car.
road legal	Safe to drive on public roads – a road legal car has passed government tests.
styling	The styling of a car is what is looks like. It is very important in sports cars and supercars.
streamlined	A very smooth shape that lets the air flow over an object. Streamlined cars go much faster than cars that are not streamlined.

More resources

Books

Supercars, Richard Nicholls, Grange Books plc
(ISBN 1-84013-501-8)
There are 300 cars in this book. Each car has a picture and
information.

Sports Cars, Designed for Success series, Ian Graham,
Heinemann Library (0-431-16563-7)
This book tells you about the design of fast cars.

Magazines

There are lots of magazines about cars. Here are two for you to try.

EVO, Dennis Publishing Ltd

Octane (classic and performance cars), Octane Media

Websites

http://www.channel4.com/4car/index.html
This Channel 4 site has news, road tests and info on the best cars
in class.

http://www.bbc.co.uk/topgear/
The BBC site for the TV series Top Gear.

Video/DVD

Jeremy Clarkson – Top 100 Cars (2001) (Cat. No. VCD0184)
Supercars and sports cars ... and a few surprises, too!

The World's Fastest Cars (1995) (Cat. No. DMDVD3569)
Plenty of fast car action.

Answers

1 A roof that folds back

2 A brand of car

3 Its doors look like wings when they are open

4 The M1

5 A charging bull

6 Volkswagen Golf GTi

7 3

8 Gold

9 124 mph

10 3.7 seconds

Index